memories and musings

a collection of poems inspired by my heavenly husband

Donna M Loftus

Contents

Prelude

There were more than 1,000 people at my husband's honorary funeral mass. Our priest, Father Duy, said he wished he could command that kind of presence on Sundays.

Memories and Musings A Collection of Poems Inspired By My Heavenly Husband / Donna M Loftus —1st ed.

ISBN Paperback 979-8-9856472-0-4

ISBN Hardback 979-8-9856472-1-1

ISBN Ebook 979-8-9856472-2-8

Images copyright Freepik, Flatiron, smalllikeart, Made by Made, tulpahn, Wanicon, iconixar, Victoruler, nawicon, srip, Nikita Golubev

Written in memory of my angel, Jeffrey Thomas Loftus.

September 17, 1958 – September 29, 2018

I promised to love you till death do us part but nothing can stop me from loving you with my whole heart.

Born Good

**(A family friend said it best at
my husband's celebration of
life, "Jeff was just born good.")**

My husband, Jeff Loftus, was just born good
Understood?

One AM phone call from a buddy with leaky pipes
No hesitation, out the door, zero gripes
Fishing a neighbor's Bible out of the grimy sewer
Makeshift coat hanger, swift maneuver — always the doer

Ford F150 ablaze in our front driveway
Hugs and humor to keep us from disarray
His famous line, "I put a lot of fires out today," came to fruition
Coming to the rescue on another precarious mission

Contractors calling on a relaxing Saturday night
Owner of Aliso Air he would easily rectify their plight
His demeanor repeatedly calm, cool, and collected
Not a hint of irritation ever detected

His daughters knew who to call when in dire straits
Dad to the rescue no matter what fate awaits
Friends would often comment WWJD
Instinctually, inexplicably he ALWAYS knew

He lived his life in action perpetually lending a hand
So now you understand
My husband, Jeff Loftus, was just born good
Understood.

Slow Pitch

Watching your slow pitch softball game
I didn't even know your name
Cute, muscular, outfielder you quickly caught my eye
Strange thought — "I'm going to marry this guy."

My delirious brain — "Are you insane?!"

The buzz in the air was wedding chatter
Background noise, "Hey batter, batter!"
Sue and Doug, the lucky pair
Love was definitely in the air

So naturally I queried the pretty blonde I had met that night
"Are you getting married soon? Have you found Mr. Right?"
Little did we both know,
I would be taking her beau

Divine intervention I would say
As I met my future husband that fortuitous day

Love Story Part I

I was working as a waitress in Elmer's Bar when I met you
Magnetic smile, crystal blue eyes, butterflies — I instantly knew
You would frequent the local hot spot, especially Happy Hour
I would bring free beers and perhaps a whiskey sour

Our mutual college friends' nuptials were quickly approaching
"When are YOU getting married?" I playfully asked, pardon my broaching
"Soon as I meet the right girl," your quick response
I smiled knowingly feigning nonchalance

I was the maid of honor at my best friend's much anticipated wedding
Palos Verdes Country Club the most sumptuous setting
Our exes Dennis and Kathy were no longer
After much imbibing I was feeling stronger

I was giddy as I asked you to dance
Pure fate or happenstance?
Later, we partied and shimmied on the historic Queen Mary
Kissed and cuddled riding home on the late-night ferry, legendary

My dad pried, "Why can't you meet a nice guy like the one I met last night?"
Unbeknownst to him, we had both found Mr. Right

Love Story Part II

Fast forward six months of blissful dating
Our courtship started accelerating
Even after I shared my tumultuous life
You still wanted to make me your future wife

Well, after many festive cocktails at a Christmas party in 1983
I seduced you into passionate unprotected sex with me
(This is how our remarkable first born, Nicole Marie, came to be!)

Although the news was surprising you took it in stride
"I knew you were the one and I want to walk on the wild side"

You didn't hesitate to get down on one knee
Pledging your unconditional love at Chart House for eternity
Storybook endings do come true
I knew this when I met you

We were the perfect balance
This was no silly dalliance
I was the excitable to your serene
Clearly, fate did intervene

Taco Bell Nights

Taco Bell ringing in my mind
Can we just press rewind?
To simple times with hungry eager faces
Spent at one of our favorite places

Two item limit, no soda, just water
Our usual Friday fodder
Nacho Supreme, no sour cream
No onions, either, comes a scream!

$4.80 to feed our family of six
Best deal in town for our weekly fix
Oh, for the good old days
Uncomplicated black and white — no greys

TGIF

Friday nights in Rancho Santa Margarita
Livin' the Dolce Vita

Hootie and the Blowfish on repeat
Kids dancing wildly to the beat
"Glass Houses" blaring thanks to Billy Joel
Can't stop won't stop good old rock 'n' roll

Homemade pizzas tossed high in the air
Scrumptious, typical Happy Hour fare
Basketball bouncing — one on one
Neighbors gathering, summertime fun

Sippin' wine in the cul-de-sac
Please, can we just go back?

Family Vacations

Three requirements for our family vacations
Pools, breakfast and Happy Hour libations
Traveling with four daughters could be ambitious
Overall, these experiences were quite auspicious

Grand Canyon studio room for our family of six
Crammed like sardines, constant flutter kicks
Our baby sick with a cough and fever of 102
Trip cut short ending up with men in G-strings at Havasu

Bass Lake on our beloved Willow Cove
Dadio's floppy hat, Ray-Bans, the speedboat he drove
Yelling "Hit it" as you popped up in the wake
No matter how many efforts it would take

Bassathon, Flip Cup, horseshoes, poker and *The Great Outdoors*
Game nights, stargazing, beersbee with Dad's favorite — Coors
Lazy days sunning, kayaking and swimming
Family and friend dinners, sunset skies as light is dimming

Yosemite in Uncle Tony's Winnebago motorhome
Car sickness, ruckus and windy roads to roam
Bear sightings in the nearby pup tent
Adding another adventuresome element

Hiking with four antsy girls in new boots
Blisters erupting amidst sister disputes
Only one made the ascent to Vernal Fall
Lindsey's triumph as she would tell all

Hyatt Regency in lush Maui
Father's Day upgraded — wowie!
Twisty turny water slide, idyllic lagoon
Squeals of elation, girls over the moon

Loftus Farms, your Dadio's roots
Riding on tractors, picking delectable fruits
Meeting cousins speaking in their Indiana drawl
"It's gonna be knee-high by the 4th of July, y'all"

Atlantis Bahamas Resort a magical place
Water park, cornrows , reggae music to embrace
Aqua blue water in the clear ocean bays
Swimming with the electrifying manta rays

Hot sweltering days at the condo in Palm Springs
Flips by Dadio in the pool, the giggles it would bring
Painted Canyon Trails in the blistering desert sun
Dad cajoling his daughter's "C'mon girls isn't this fun?"

Melty popsicles eaten on the golf course
Ball flying at Jenna's knee in full force
Popster, livid, mad as a hornet's nest
Finding his granddaughter's culprit his only quest

Day excursions to the tide pools at illustrious Laguna Beach
Poking urchins and sea anemones — the lessons they would teach
Ending with ice cream cones and sticky fingers
Soaking up the summer fun while it lingers

Loftus party of six in a pint size minivan
Milan is where our escapades began
Colorful vodka drinks at the famed Ice Bar
Fur hats feeling like a prominent czar

Driving on mountainous terrain, trying Dad's nerves
Lake Como roads and their many twists and curves
Bougainvillea arches abound in this elegant city so pristine
Our boisterous family sipping wine and relishing local cuisine

Meeting friends for Easter in renowned Florence
Pillowy pockets of gnocchi, flavor so intense
Limoncello shots with owners at a cozy, hidden trattoria
While the Santa Maria del Fiore Cathedral belted out "Gloria"

French fries on pizzas and beers from a vending machine
Paderno del Grappa the ultimate college scene
Jenna's home for her semester abroad
The meandering streets of Venice we trod

Family vacations could be challenging, but we have no regret
Etched in our minds and hearts, memories we will never forget

Switzerland

On magical snow-laden Switzerland streets
We were famished and craving fine Suisse eats
The quaint restaurant appeared as if in a dream
With its cobblestone exterior and storybook theme

Overlooking the charming town square
Visions of snowflakes falling everywhere
Tiny drapes adorned our cozy booth
I was sipping Petite Arvine and you, vermouth — so couth

The Bechamel lasagna was absolutely decadent
Each meal thereafter an unachievable precedent
The drapes were drawn and without a doubt we were frisky
But we handled ourselves with aplomb, other actions would be
risky

Breathing in the sights, the sounds, the tantalizing smells
In the distance the church steeple's clanging bells
The most romantic night in a fairytale setting
Painted in my mind, never forgetting

Royalty

A marathon in Paris was on my bucket list
Aw but the memory of our castle tryst
I would have missed

Drinking copious amounts of luscious French wine
Party boat cruising the River Rhine
You are all mine

I'll spare you the details
Just know that love prevails

Heads pounding exploring the picturesque countryside
Discovering the MOST scrumptious Monte Cristo on our
bike ride

What I wouldn't give for one more kiss,
One more night of marital bliss

Arabian Nights

Desert safari in Dubai
Miles of sand piled high

Camel rides, Jeeps on the dunes
Giddy beneath the Arabian moons

Smoking hookah with our newfound friends, stunning Nigerian
newlyweds
Adorned with intricate headwear in colorful threads

Feasting, dancing, henna tattoos
Night of wonder, golden hour hues

Freude

Munich Oktoberfest 2010
How I remember when

Clinking steins, chanting "Prost"
Overflowing beers, German toast

Lederhosen sightings everywhere
Running amok, not a care

Festival tents filled with life
Carefree hubby, happy wife

Bratwurst sizzling on the grill
World of merriment, standing still

Ferris wheel joy ride over the sight
Making out in the heat of the night

Double thick French fries eaten in bed
End to a perfect day, enough said

Amalfi

Motor scootin' on the suspended Amalfi Coast
Father, Son and Holy Ghost!
(Ultimate trust in my hubby foremost)

Intoxicating, iridescent sea
Breathtaking beauty, free
Wind whipping through my hair
Tasting the salty air

Pin turn curves
Full of nerves
Aromatic wine on the hilltop of Ravello
Balmy, fine and mellow

Beverly Hills
Shenanigans

Vodka bar, ridiculous fur coats
Sowing some middle age, wild oats
One shot, two shots, three shots, four
We're not feeling it let's do one more

Happy Hour — why the hell not?
Beverly Hills show us what you got
We need food and a bottle of wine
Italian anyone? Sounds divine

Inhaling focaccia with intoxicated grins
Laughter and pasta along with the spins
Morning after, heads like lead
Can we just stay in bed?

Need coffee and bagels ASAP
Larry King is that you we see?
A night for the books, unbridled fun
Besties forever, second to none

Shattered

Beautiful Saturday for a bike and a run
Crisp leaves, cool, bright autumn sun
Cannondale jersey in the most vibrant hue
Magnifying your eyes, baby blue

"Spray the f@cking crickets" shouted in haste
Such unwitting words to waste
Flying down the street
Running buddy to meet

Joyful banter, third daughter's wedding week
So excited I can hardly speak
Elated you are enjoying your mountain ride
Sense of happiness soon belied, as I go inside

Better check my phone before I blend my shake
911 texts? There must be some mistake
Unconscious, heart, he's still fighting
Flicker of hope igniting

Shock, confusion, green light
Dear God, let him be all right
Wires, monitors, can't stabilize
Shouts of desperate cries

"Thank you, thank you" while whispering my eternal "I love you"
No response. Beeping sounds. Stat. Code blue.
Doctor's words, nothing more we could do...

I crumble to the ground
Moaning guttural sound
Time stands still
Your body so cold, surreal

I come home to our living room mirror arcanely shattered
Depicting my life in ruins unfathomably shattered

Morning Awakening

I reach for you in the morning and the evening — you are not there
Your soul dances, now, in the wispy clouds of air
You are forever changed and so am I
As I gaze at your radiant beauty in the brilliant, heavenly sky

I am awed by the splendor of your magnificent celestial space
I can only imagine the pure joy of meeting Jesus face to face
Our grandbabies look to find you in the darkness of the night
There you are, "Poppi's Star," shining ever so bright

My heart aches for you, my precious husband, in your familiar
form
I pray to God for strength to weather this grievous storm
I see you in our beautiful daughters as they choose to find hope
amidst their tears
You comfort them with your gentle presence, calming all their fears

Your character shines in our sons-in-law wisely chosen, and the one
yet to be
As the Lord and you refine him "Perfectly Imperfect" for your
precious baby
You will be cherished and loved infinitely all the days of my life
I am forever grateful and honored that I was YOUR wife

Love Letters
Unwritten

Love letters appearing in the oddest of places
Filling my soul with their subtle graces
Unconditional love shown right from the start
Surrounding me with peace and stealing my heart

"Love Letters" inscribed on a planter box
Your witty humor obvious and so dearly unorthodox
An email sent after a fun-filled night in Prague, and one I will
always cherish
The lightness and laughter, the knowing our love would never
perish

Helping hands given to family and friends
Always willing, a love note that transcends
Yes, your love letters were not written with paper or pen
But witnessed in your daily life over and over again

Numerous lives touched with hardly a word
Your selfless voice undeniably heard
Now you write me love letters from the heavens on high
Unceasing love tethered to the breathless sky

Father's Day

Hidden boxes filled with stories
Adventures and memorabilia of your Dadio's glories
A love letter written from me to you
Forever yours, my dream come true

Poppi's bats, Poppi's bases
Broadest smiles on our grandchildren's faces
Softball game played in your loving memory
Balls flying, kids running amok, carefree

Ballpark pizza and Coors Light beers
"Happy Father's Day" to you we cheers
Joyful banter, reflections abound
We feel your presence all around

Year One

365 days, 12 months, 1 year
Birthdays, anniversaries, holidays
How we long to hold you near

Our hearts are broken as we search for air
You are nowhere to be found, yet you are everywhere
Your undeniable presence infusing a wedding so divine
The floodgates of heaven were opened in God's jubilant design

Crickets chirping in the light of day
Showing up in places they never may
Your sense of humor clearly stated
My final words to you plainly fated

"Brandy" being played at the most befitting times
Memories of your piano fingers, so sublime
The beauty that surrounds us and permeates our being
Glimpses of paradise, in you, we are clearly seeing

The grandbabies gaze at the sunset and squeal with delight,
"Look, Nonni, look! Poppi painted the sky tonight!"
Your baby blues peeking through a sliver in the cloud
Eyes shining so bright, ever so proud

We feel you as the seasons change and the breeze turns crisp
and cool
A gentle reminder of our year of firsts, our blessed renewal
You wrap your arms around us in the comfort of our family and
friends
Their encouraging words and acts of kindness heal our hearts and
mends

Because of you, my beloved husband, we are loved beyond measure
Your precious soul lives on; a gift we will always treasure
A family friend said it best, "Jeff was just born good"
And so, we go forth as we know you would

Heads held high with hope, courage and grace
Knowing you are smiling upon us in your eternal resting place

#Girldad

He was the best #girldad before it was even cool
In our house the unspoken "Girls ALWAYS rule"
He had not one Daddy's girl, but four
Squeals of delight as he walked through the door

"Trying for the boy?" commonly heard by a passerby
"Nope, I always wanted four girls" his staunch reply
He carried your picture wherever he went
Full of pride and joy, his loving sentiment.

He taught you about Lefty Loosey and Righty Tighty
All about faith and the Lord God Almighty
He preached, "If you don't have anything nice to say, don't say
anything at all"
How to throw and catch a Hail Mary football

Give a firm handshake with confidence
Greet others with genuine providence
Do your chores and heed his unwavering warning
Or you will find yourself car washing at the dawn of Monday
morning

Empty threats were clearly not his style
Remember when you all walked home from church a mile?
5 AM practices for morning swim
Obviously don't ask Mom — ask him

Extended back rubs on a good night
Stories abound his ritual rite
"Boyfriends aren't all they're cracked up to be,
There are so many other fish in the sea!"

Asked how he managed conversations about the birds and the bees
His big smile as he replied, "I'm on a need-to-know basis — my
wife handles these!"
In his eyes you were all pure and innocent
No need to entertain worry or discontent

He instilled hard work and giving back
Be on time — do not slack
Tide pools, angel games, family vacations
He gave you all rock-solid foundations

"Life isn't fair," never so true
As we navigate life without you
When it comes to #girldads we were infinitely blessed
You were simply the absolute BEST

Love ya
Dad

Sixty

Allow me to wallow in a little self-pity
As turning 60 without my hubby has not been pretty
He was always willing to hear my complaints
Now he's too busy conversing with saints

Backyard BBQ, innocent bug bite on my face
Then came rheumatologists, IRS theft, and my fall from grace
A swelling thumb could be life threatening
Seriously! What would the New Year bring?

Four sties in my eye — why?
Cellulitis again, I cry
More antibiotics and shots in my rear
What new anomaly will now appear?

Diagnosis of bleeding ulcers, no tomatoes, citrus, or red wine
Don't worry, with my current monk-like status, I'll be fine
I know with family and friends I am abundantly blessed
So please pardon me while I get this off my chest

Excuse me for all my ranting and raving
I think it's a Kamikaze shot I am craving
I long for a dive bar and dancing on the table
I may be down but I'm not out — catch me when I'm able

COVID-19

We wear masks and live in unpredictable chaos
As I struggle to process your profound loss
Such an unrecognizable place
How I long to talk to you face to face

The world is being threatened by COVID-19
Archenemy lurking, sight unseen
Social distancing now the norm
While we weather this dubious storm

Fear and suspicion plague our once normal days
Perhaps the answer lies in creating new ways?
Looking through the lens of what really matters
Even though it appears life is in shatters

Simple pleasures often taken for granted
Political views left and right slanted
A gentle hug, a soft tender kiss
This is what I really miss

Year Two

Year two reality has slowly crept in
No longer numb, in a tailspin
The joy, the sorrow, the pain
Will I ever be whole again?

2020 such a strange year
COVID-19, masks, hysterical fear
Kobe and Gianna's tragic deaths
Aching reminder of your last breaths

Health challenges, identity theft with the IRS
Life upended, an erratic mess
I long for your comfort in the heat of the night
Whispering "Everything will be all right"

I rented the same beach house on Chinquapin
I thought you had been
My mind plays tricks with the before and after
The longing for your belly laughter

My poem got published in Jenna's zine
Sights of Oktoberfest, unforgettable scene
Two precious grandbabies will be born soon
Reflecting Poppi's star shining by the moon

You now exist in a sacred realm
Forever you will be at our helm
I miss you more each passing day
As I go forward into the unforeseen fray

Runs

Runs for 40 years — Cheers!

Runs to stoke my creative mind
My very favorite kind
Runs praying the rosary, blasting "rock n' roll"
Energizing my body, feeding my soul

Runs to keep my peace and sanity
And perhaps fueling my vanity
Runs to burn more calories
Definitely not a fan of these

Runs to ease the pain
For the solace I gain
Runs to process my grief
When I can't feel the ground underneath

Runs to glimpse the brilliant sunrise
God's glory witnessed in the dawn skies
Runs to heal my broken heart
My love surpasses ''till death do us part"

Runs on the plains of Africa during the migration
Monkeys eyeing me quizzically in this wild nation
Runs at a 10-miler in scenic Amsterdam
And through the royal streets of Buckingham

Runs on the infamous coast of Bondi Beach
A slice of heaven within my reach
Runs on the concrete Maltese pavement
Historical sites surrounding me with amazement

Runs on the outer edges of Punta Arenas
Conversing with the local Argentinas
Runs through castles in the Dubrovnik countryside
While scaling the path on the Adriatic seaside

Runs with good friends for 30 years
The camaraderie, laughter and the tears
Too many races to count, marathons galore
Probably 13 but who's keeping score?

Runs to prove I won't quit
At 61 I still got grit
Runs until my feet won't move
Until then, catch me in my groove

Trader Joe's

Honey, I know you will laugh at my story
Your wild Italian wife in all her glory
How I wish you were there with me

I went to Trader Joe's today and noticed a sign on the door —
Fully vaccinated patrons don't need to wear masks anymore!
Well, Alleluia and Glory Be
I tore that mask right off — "I'm free"

I whizzed around the store like a bat out of hell
My jubilation no common clerk could quell
Up and down each aisle I slowly strolled
I felt so empowered, so unbelievably bold

I was grinning from ear to ear for all the world to see
Caught in the pure joy of my maskless, mini shopping spree

Night

I come home alone again
A familiar place I have been
Deafening silence fills the air
Memories of you everywhere

I shout, "Alexa, on!"
You are still gone
I eat dinner with a candle lit
Gracing the spot, you used to sit

I mindlessly watch Gilmore Girls then drag myself to bed
The moment I always dread — my mind swirling with all things
left unsaid
I reach for you in the still of the night
Hopeful you'll come in my dreams until daylight

Morning

I arise early with gratitude for a new day
Meditate with my Calm app and begin to pray
I meander downstairs for my morning brew
My non-negotiable — not just one but two

I read my devotionals, sift through my emails
Eager for a new dawn and what it entails, especially the iconic
Nordstrom sales!
I peruse my Instagram for new recipes
Influencers — aka Half Baked Harvest and her specialties

My daily routine, finding my peace
The blessings that never cease
I lace up my shoes and head out for my run
Thankful for another trip around the sun

The Big 3-0

Our favorite thing about our baby, Michelle Lynn
Where do we even begin?
Your giving and loving heart
This is where we will start

Your beauty radiates deeply from within
Light shining everywhere you have been
Always going the extra mile
Yummy cookies that make us smile

Steadfast faith that never falters
Even when life undeniably alters
Finding peace in the sunset sky
Small tattoo, the reason why

Dadio noted your attention to detail at a young age
Your bright mind already so incredibly sage
Sarcastic humor and classic dry wit —
Hmmm... I wonder where you got it?

Your adventuresome spirit has taken on new heights
Road trippin', Colorado Springs, Taos trailer nights
Maybe you'll be the face of Rip Curl
With your latest undertaking — "Surfer Girl"

So many favorite things we love about you
Just one would never do
Our Baby Meesh is turning the Big 3-0
Where on earth did the time go?

This is your decade, you're ready to soar
Always remember we couldn't love you more

P.S. I'm on my 3rd novena for Mr. Perfectly Imperfect to show his face
He best be one phenomenal human to handle your beauty, strength and grace!

ME

Older, wiser, and free
Who should I be?
An esoteric, sarcastic poet
Maybe I am and just don't know it

Recipe developer on Instagram
Momma Donna famous blogger — hot damn!
Life coach encompassing mind, body, and soul
Teaching others how to achieve their goal

Don't stop me now I'm on a roll!

Substitute teacher as I've been in the past
Sorry I don't want to be masked
Should I retire, play pickleball and do lunch
Drink Bloody Marys and travel a bunch?

I felt empowered with you by my side
My gentle, supportive, loving guide
I know you're always there lighting the way
Still, I wonder what would you say?

It's hard to know what to do
With the ME without you

THEY

Do you ever listen to **THEY** and what **THEY** say??

Don't eat this and don't eat that
Eat less carbs and eat more fat — imagine that!
Vegan, keto, gluten-free,
THEY think **THEY** are the boss of me

Include more fiber, protein, and add wheatgrass
Well, **THEY** can just kiss my Italian ass
My apologies again I must go to mass

THEY also say time will heal
THEY don't see the pain I feel
THEY remark, "Get a dog, it would be so good for you"
Apparently **THEY** don't know who **THEY** are talking to

I have occasionally fallen prey to **THEY** I must confess
However, short term solutions don't equate to long term success
THEY will continue with their paradoxical spews
My response is now Fake News!

I've realized in my 61 years **THEY** are wrong,
The answers have resided in **ME** all along

Year Three

This is the time of year when summer ends
And miracle month transcends
Three years of celebrating your "Angelversary"
September lovingly holds your memory

Your birth. Your death. The joy. The pain.
The autumn sun. The wind and rain.
Grief, a tangled web of emotions that constantly collide
The forever longing to have you by our side

I love you and miss you endlessly my heavenly hubby

You're My Best Friends

One is my sister-in-law, one a family friend
All of us sisters in the end
My ride or dies, my constant support
Undoubtedly the best threesome cohort

We are there for each other in the happy and sad
Ever so thankful for our perfect triad
We are Charlie's Angels, Las Tres Amigas
Anyone who witnesses our banter wants to be us

Rolling in laughter until our stomachs hurt
Over our BFF's stiff collared, white preppy shirt
No matter our conversations — serious or mundane
These exchanges lighten our mood and keep us sane

Religiously we celebrate birthday dinners at "Nick's"
Light and fluffy topics, no provoking politics
Butter cake and gelato an absolute must
The melt in your mouth pleasure, for this we lust

We often dine at "Hanna's," "Tutto's," or "Roger's Gardens"
The location irrelevant as our unison always heartens
We may sometimes disagree, but we're always in sync
Especially after partaking in a tasty, intoxicating drink

Wherever we go, whatever we do
I can't imagine life without you two
You make my world a better place
You put a permanent smile on my face

Crickets

Unknowingly, my final words to my husband were "Spray the f*cking crickets!"
Needless to say, in his humorous way, he never forgets — I have copious regrets
Although I have no excuse for the profanities I uttered
There is a history for why they were muttered

Backtrack to 1984 when we were newly married
Crickets had invaded our house, I was justly harried
Months went by before they were finally under control
As you can see this disturbing experience took its toll

You will always have the final word now as evidenced by your cricket sightings
Your supernatural abilities abound in the following uncanny writings
Although unbelievable they are all legit
Justifiably your spirit animal is a cricket

On your daughter Lindsey's wedding rehearsal night
The room was dark, lit only by candlelight
Your father rose from his seat
Moving everyone to their feet

In the dim silence, after his poignant speech
The harmonious sound of crickets within reach
You were there in that room, no denying
The solace we felt indisputably mystifying

The morning of the ceremony on a run with Nicole
Crickets were heard in unison, again to soothe our soul
Mountain bikers pedaled naively by
As we reveled in our concert from the sky

A Jerusalem cricket so very rare
Residing on Michelle's Bible study chair
A common cricket holding space for weeks in Jenna's art class
Your audacious spirit comforting and filled with amusing sass

A cricket appearing on our best friend's Happy Hour glass
Instead of frolicking in the nearby grass
Your bold presence felt with full force
Never one to miss a party, of course

A solo cricket jumping out of Lindsey's unpacked suitcase
Surprise for your daughter's thirtieth, the smile on her face
Live crickets on our Christmas tree
You've gone too far, obviously!

Hopping out of Craig's backpack on the highway
Just stopping by to tell his good friend "Hi"
Spider cricket picture shown randomly in a Taos dive bar
Sending your baby girl comfort from afar

Filled with sadness on your third "Angelversary"
So lonely, just wanting you there with me
Outside of Nordstrom I heard the familiar chirping sound
Incredulously in the bathroom stall there was a cricket crawling around

Poppi cricket sounds here and there
If we look and listen you are everywhere
Thankful for the many visits that will never cease
Your playful antics bringing us unending peace

Unseated By the Toilet

I was unseated by the toilet one brisk winter day
As a replacement was needed, my mind went astray
The last time we purchased a commode was 1995
When Jenna's toy princess took a nosedive

There it sat obstructing the flow
Water backed up, no place to go
My eyes teared up at the memories
While the plumber rattled off varieties

Adaptive, oval, round or high
You would know which kind to buy
Enter my angel on earth, Chris, my husband's brother
These Loftus men are like no other

Within hours sitting in my backyard was a latrine
The most comical sight I've ever seen
My grief melted as I laughed out loud
To my new throne I reverently bowed

You Would Be So Proud

Year three... An update on our family

Our Daughters

Nicole continues to thrive as an accomplished professor at
Saddleback
Her confidence has soared, as she is deservedly on the tenure track
Working full time, raising two kids, surgery with foot in a boot
Still a highly efficient five-foot-one dynamo, there is no dispute

Jenna is currently working on her fourth zine
Editor of these artistic visions to be seen
Her soulful postings are wisdom of pearls
Stealing time, while caring for her three little girls

Lindsey immersed herself in Stratton's spectacular 1st birthday
celebration
Pondering if her career as an occupational therapist could unite
with her fascination
Her blissful talent presently knitting adorable baby beanies galore
Announcing her family will be growing to Lodge party of four!

Michelle has changed her position to product manager at Q'Apel
Combining her speech and language degree with business, she is
sure to excel
Her limits have been pushed far outside her comfort zone
Adventuring, seeking, growing, risking the unknown

Our SONS (Sons-in-Law)

James is now in charge of the Mission Hospital Neuro and
Spine Unit
With his intelligence, kindness and compassion, he is the perfect fit
In addition to his nurse practitioner and business degrees
He's a rad dad and soccer coach while dabbling in Realtor licensees

Ryan, iconic regional sales manager at Thor
Continually impresses as motorhome sales soar
A seasoned, dedicated #girldad of three
Earning his stars and stripes as stellar Daddy

Brandon as always unruffled, jovial and collected
Juggling MBA projects, fatherhood, and Verathon, unaffected
Dedicated profusely to his baby boy
Relishing his new role with immeasurable joy

Our Grandchildren

Trent Loftus and Maisley Christine started kindergarten in the fall
I revisit these times and vividly remember them all
Briella Marie and Coura Joan enjoying preschool
Learning the alphabet and the Golden Rule

Trent, a bright, sensitive boy with a loving heart
His passions include athletics and drawing colorful art
Briella, an independent mini might with a strong plié
She is a sweetheart, a giver and her hugs make my day

Maisley, a beautiful perceptive soul who delights in make believe
Her imaginative world is where her tender emotions find their
reprieve
Coura, our determined, tousled hair, fearless flyer
So lovable, with her gravelly voice yelling "Higher, higher!"

Two more miracles born this past year
Your namesakes, Stratton Jeffrey and Mara Jeffries, so dear

Stratton, an adorable, toothy grinned, curious explorer, now one
Fills us with warmth, his sweet disposition as bright as the sun
Mara, with her peaceful presence and twinkly blue eyes
Her calm, inviting smile that enlivens the skies

We recently learned we will be grandparents to seven
I see your beaming face smiling widely from heaven
Our precious grandchildren, blessings from above
Their tiny beings emanating love

Me, I'm finally writing my book
61 years was all it took!
You were my divine inspiration
Now I'm going on a dreamy wellness vacation

Epilogue

My angel, Jeff Loftus, left an indelible imprint on all who knew him. I was honored to call him my husband for almost 35 years. The unconditional love and devotion he showed to his family and friends is immortal. The endless memories we created were the impetus for finally writing my book. He will forever be my soulmate and divine inspiration.

Grief is a tangled web of emotions that constantly collide. Joy and sorrow. Despair and faith. I hope my words resonate with you, bringing you solace and strength as you reflect on your own personal grief journey. You are not alone. Our loved ones live on eternally etched in our hearts.

I am forever grateful to my daughters, my "tough cookies," Nicole, Jenna, Lindsey, and Michelle. Without their constant love and gentle nudging, this book would not have been written. Thank you to my sons (in-law), James, Ryan, and Brandon; so wisely chosen. Their support and loyalty is incomparable. My precious grandchildren, Trent, Maisley, Briella, Coura, Stratton, Mara, and blessing to be, light up my life.

. . .

I am so appreciative of my family and friends who lift me up every day.

Finally, thank you to Lindsey Smith and Alex Franzen. These dynamic young women helped my tiny book become a reality. They have a special gift of connection and making words come to life. Also, many thanks to the Get It Done production team, Woz Flint, Andrew Fox, Kayla Floyd, and Lucy Giller, who helped complete my book journey.

About the Author

Donna Loftus is an energetic and resilient people-person who resides in sunny Southern California. She is blessed with four daughters, three sons (in-law), and her soon to be seven grandchildren who affectionately call her "Nonni." Her heavenly hubby was the calm to her feisty.

Her morning coffee is non-negotiable, and her runs are sacred. She has trotted all over the globe with her husband, landing just shy of seven continents.

Thanks in large part to her full-blooded Italian heritage, Donna is slightly obsessed with collecting new recipes and creating specialties of her own. Making her traditional meat sauce is a labor of love and always cause for a celebration.

On occasion she is known to throw back a Kamikaze shot and get low on the dance floor to her favorite song, "You Shook Me All Night Long." Her love of books has been apparent from a young age when she read the Collier's Encyclopedias for fun. Nowadays she appreciates a sappy rom-com and sometimes a good survivor tale, like *Educated*.

After many rewarding years as a full-time mom and educator, she is expanding her horizons.

Her faith, boisterous family, and loyal friends feed her soul, keep her sane, and helped her write this book. Sixty-one years is all it took!

Lightning Source UK Ltd.
Milton Keynes UK
UKHW010635090522
402703UK00001B/83